on the Inside

Reducing Recidivism Through Behavioral Change

Dean Collinwood
Foreword by Sean Covey

© FranklinCovey Co. All Rights Reserved.

No part of this book may be reproduced, in any form or by any means, without permission in writing from the publisher. Requests to the publisher for permission should be addressed to the Rights Manager, FranklinCovey Co., 2200 W. Parkway Blvd., Salt Lake City, Utah 84119, (801) 817-1776, email: legal@franklincovey.com.

Company and product names mentioned herein are the trademarks or registered trademarks of their respective owners. Published by FranklinCovey Publishing, a division of FranklinCovey Co.

ISBN 978-1-936111-20-6

Printed in the United States of America.

Acknowledgements

With thanks to Jerry Gasko for having the vision.

Contents

Foreword 1

Chapter 1: The Challenge 3

Chapter 2: Attempts to Reform Prisoners 11

Chapter 3: 7 *Habits* Programs for Adult Offenders 15
    The 7 *Habits* in Collier County, Florida
    The 7 *Habits* in a California Women's Prison
    The 7 *Habits* in Other Prison Settings

Chapter 4: Using the 7 *Habits* to Reduce Juvenile
          Recidivism in the United States 24

Chapter 5: The Chrysalis Program™ and the
          7 *Habits* in the United Kingdom 27

Chapter 6: Individual Inmate Application of the
          7 *Habits* for Behavioral Change 32

Chapter 7: What Have We Learned?
          Where Do We Go From Here? 36

Notes 40

Index 43

Foreword

Ever since my book *The 7 Habits of Highly Effective Teens* hit the bookstores in 1998, I have watched with surprise and gratitude as countless teenagers worldwide have used its principles to resist negative peer pressure, make smarter decisions, and live up to their potential. Even more surprising to me has been how numerous elementary schools around the globe have adopted the *7 Habits* as an operating system inside their schools and are successfully teaching these principles to kids even as young as five years old.

I am aware, however, that far too many have not had the benefit of early exposure to the life-changing guidance found in the *7 Habits* concepts, such as responsibility, vision, teamwork, and renewal. Some of them, unfortunately, will spend years in prison because of bad decisions made early in life. So why not take advantage of their incarceration to teach them the *7 Habits* and mentor them while they take their first tentative steps back to society? Why not use these principles to change their worldviews in prison so that they will be less likely to re-offend after they are released?

That is what *7 Habits on the Inside* argues for. Written by professor and Fulbright Scholar Dr. Dean Collinwood, *7 Habits on the Inside* demonstrates with empirical evidence as well as testimonials that inmate behavior can and does change when the *7 Habits* principles are taught and applied. Collinwood recognizes that all the evidence is not in, and that there is much more to do to fully substantiate the arguments he makes. Yet, as he says, "the preliminary evidence makes a strong enough case" for the *7 Habits* to justify their adoption in prisons everywhere.

I am, perhaps, less cautious than Professor Collinwood; I know the *7 Habits* make a big difference for ordinary teens and teens in trouble. As well, I have seen the *7 Habits* transform the lives of numerous people, from moms and dads to teachers and CEOs, from elementary and high schools to multibillion-dollar companies. So why not try them out on inmates? As I see it, the cost of *7 Habits* training for inmates pales in comparison to the enormous financial burden society bears when released convicts offend again and again.

This is a book that should be read by every prison administrator and every government official whose portfolio includes the criminal justice system. I believe the book will guide them to actions that will make their jobs a lot easier—and society a lot safer.

Sean Covey
July 2010

1

The Challenge

Everyone involved with criminal justice knows that measuring recidivism is a "sticky wicket." Does one declare a former convict "cured" if he or she remains out of prison for one year after release? two years? three years? Do we not have to wait until the ex-convict dies to make the claim with complete confidence that he or she never again returned to a life of crime?

What about the matter of jurisdiction? A parolee or probationer may never return to prison in the same locality or country in which he committed his first offense and would thus be defined as a "non-recidivist." But what if he offends in another country or another part of the country? Is the worldwide tracking of offenders sophisticated enough to account for all offenders over the entirety of their lives, wherever they live?

We are aware of these and other problems associated with making claims about recidivism rates. But we are also aware that the current state of affairs is untenable. Over 10 million people worldwide are held in prisons, and according to a 2009 study, prison populations are on the rise in 71 percent of the countries in the world.[1] By far, the largest number of prisoners per capita is found in the United States which incarcerates offenders at a ratio five times higher than the world average; there is now approximately 1 person in prison for every 99 U.S. citizens. But the United States is certainly not the only country with large prison populations. Figure 1 gives a sampling in rounded numbers of selected prison populations.

Fig. 1
Inmate Population by Country
2009

Country	Prison Inmates
United States	2.3 million
China	1.5 million
Russia	1.0 million
Brazil	440,000
Mexico	250,000
Thailand	166,000
England, Wales, Scotland	100,000

Source: Roy Walmsley, comp. "World Prison Population List" 8th ed., International Centre for Prison Studies, King's College, London, 2009.

What is most disturbing about these large numbers of incarcerated men and women (and boys and girls) is that when they are released, approximately two-thirds of them, on average, will be re-arrested within three years, and more than half will return to prison. Be aware that these figures are only part of the story; many re-offenders are not caught a second or third time for their crimes, leaving the new victims and society as a whole to suffer the consequences without redress.

Once again, we note the difficulty of measuring global recidivism, but in the United States, a 1994 study by the U.S. Department of Justice of 272,111 prisoners released from incarceration in 15 states found that the released prisoners had accumulated 4.1 million arrest charges before their most recent incarceration and added another 744,000 charges within three years of their release[3]. Return-to-crime rates varied by type of offence, with some offences being extremely likely to be correlated with recidivism. For example, some 80 percent of motor-vehicle thieves returned to prison. For all prisoners released and tracked in this study, *67.5 percent* were rearrested within three years, and *51.8 percent* were sent back to prison.

Figure 2 shows the growth of the prison population in the United States over an 86-year period.[2]

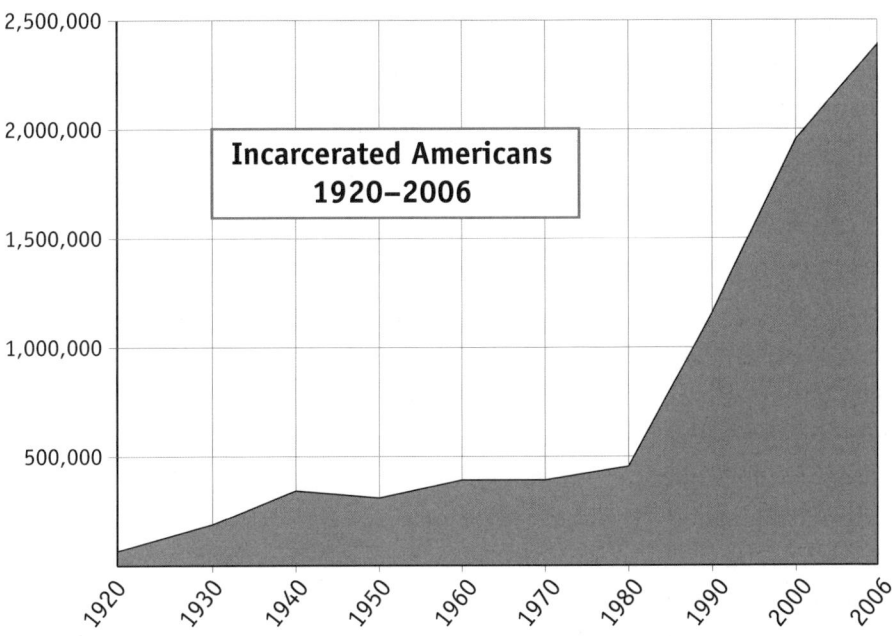

**Fig. 2
Growth of the Prison Population
in the United States
1920-2006**

Source: Justice Policy Institute Report: the Punishing Decade & U.S. Bureau of Justice Statistics Bulletin, NCJ 219416—Prisoners in 2006.

In England, the number of adult male prisoners who re-offend within two years is about 58 percent but rises to 72 percent for males ages 18–20. It is about 60 percent for adult women. Imagine the frustration of police officers and judges who repeatedly see the same offenders back in their courtrooms. "I am a magistrate," says one British judge, "but my sentences seem to generate more crime."[4]

In Canada, the readmission rate for 42,000 offenders released from federal prisons and tracked for 10 years thereafter (1975–1985) was an impressively low 37 percent, but whether some of them were rearrested and sent to provincial prisons was not studied (in Canada, persons sentenced to terms of two years or more serve their sentences in a federal institution, while sentences of less than two years are served in provincial institutions).[5] A similar study from 1978 to 1993 of 968 Canadian female offenders found a recidivism rate of 22 percent, although once again, only federal readmission numbers were analyzed.[6]

Like recidivism, crime rates vary by the demographic makeup of a country at a particular time (countries with large numbers of teens and people in their early 20s have higher crime rates, for example), and by many other factors, including political decisions about what constitutes a crime. Thus, recidivism and crime rates fluctuate; but what is consistent is that, worldwide, more than half of those people who break the law and are sentenced to prison will re-offend relatively soon after their release and be re-incarcerated. Prisons, it would seem, are not places where behavioral change is being successfully taught.

What does the prison system's revolving door cost society? Actual figures on the total financial impact of recidivism are impossible to calculate and vary significantly by country, region, or era. But even conservative estimates are staggering. Prisoners require, among other things, medical, dental, and mental health services, and if they are physically handicapped or elderly, they require additional help. Vocational training, drug and alcohol rehabilitation, and legal and other services occupy the time of tens of thousands of lawyers, judges, social workers, doctors, guards, prison officials, parole officers, and others involved in keeping lawbreakers off the streets. All these services must be paid for, and they are paid for by taxing law-abiding citizens and businesses.

The cost of crime also includes replacing stolen and damaged property, providing medical and psychological treatment for injured individuals, assisting torn-apart families of both victims and offenders, and coping with the incalculable, permanent trauma that ensues when lives are snuffed out by violence. (There were 14,180 murder victims in the United States in 2008 alone—and that represents a *reduction* compared to a decade ago.)[7] The U.S. Federal Bureau of Investigation estimated that in the year 1996, the fully loaded cost of crimes against persons—just one of seven major violent-crime categories—cost U.S. taxpayers $450 billion.[8]

> In one year, crimes against persons cost U.S. taxpayers $450 billion.

In the United Kingdom, the cost of dealing with the consequences of recorded crime (remember, many crimes go unreported) is over £75 billion (US$ 108 billion) a year;⁹ £10 billion (US$ 14 billion) of that comes from new crimes by offenders recently released from prison.[10] In the United States, it is thought that keeping one offender in prison for one day costs about $60 on average. That works out to $138 million a day or almost $50 billion a year. That is the national average; some states, like Michigan, report costs of $88 a day, or more than $32,000 per inmate per year.

As astounding as these figures are, they are only a fraction of the actual cost to society. When this book went to press, there were an additional 4.9 million Americans out of prison on parole or probation, which means they were still under the watchful eye of the justice system and thus still costing society large sums of money.[11] The number of former prisoners out on parole or probation often exceeds the number in prison. For example, in the U.S. state of Oregon, which claims a low 33 percent recidivism rate, there are 13,500 offenders in prison but 2.5 times that many (34,000) out on parole and still under state supervision. Some 4000 inmates are released under supervision each year in Oregon.[12]

Money for prisons does not "grow on trees"; it comes directly from citizens and businesses in the form of higher taxes. The more money spent on prisons, the less there is for other valuable activities. For instance, the Pew Charitable Trust found that, over 10 years, the inflation-adjusted rate of increase on prison spending in the United States was 127 percent, while for higher education the increase was only 21 percent.[13] Imagine how much more developed U.S. universities would be if they, like prisons, had received 127 percent funding increases over the past decade. Yet, budgets for prisons never seem to be large enough to cope with the growing prison populations. In fact, most prison administrators live with a perpetual budget crisis. This is especially true when the economy is not vibrant and tax revenues decline across the board.[14]

Many cash-strapped prison officials try to cope with their budget problems by cutting out prisoner-education programs, scaling back legal services, or reducing the number of prison staff. But with the prisoners still inside the walls, no one can ever just turn out the lights and go home. Large numbers of prison employees are continually needed to care for and monitor the inmates.

Moreover, as it turns out, reducing prison staff is a double-edged sword. For instance, one U.S. state, whose governor loudly declared that he would not add any more government workers to the state's stretched payroll, ended up paying out $67 million in overtime costs to the prison staff already employed in 2009. Why? Someone had to be on-site to keep the prisons running, so the employees simply worked more hours and at higher, overtime hourly pay rates.[15]

Unable to balance budgets through staff reductions, harried prison officials sometimes try eliminating prisoner-education programs. They say they simply cannot afford to provide such services to the inmates. But as Professor Russell W. Rumberger of the California Dropout Research Project pointed out, "Interventions pay for themselves."[16] Los Angeles County Sheriff Lee Baca agrees with Rumberger. As a law enforcement official in a city with 400 gangs and 40,000 gang members, Baca and his officers live on the front line of juvenile crime by school dropouts—crime that costs citizens in excess of $1 billion annually. But the good news from the California Dropout Research Project is that the state is realizing $2 in savings for every $1 invested in high school dropout programs.

We believe similar cost savings will be realized when inmates are given appropriate training while incarcerated—training that will help them arrive at a new paradigm for their lives and allow them to practice living within that paradigm for months or years before they are released back to society. While some prison administrators cut back on inmate training programs, others are serious enough about preparing inmates to succeed on the outside that they *increase*, not decrease, access to programs that will change inmates' worldviews and behaviors *while in prison*. If prisoners do not receive such training, they will be back in jail shortly after their release, and the budget crisis and headaches for prison administrators will never go away.

> A huge portion of the cost of crime is caused by repeat offenders.

Remember, a huge portion of the costs associated with new crimes is generated by offenders who have already served time for earlier crimes. In the United States, it is estimated that by 2011, over 2000 inmates, on average, will be released from prison back into their communities *every day,* with some states releasing many more, and others less. *The majority of them will re-offend.* Imagine the dramatic decline in the tax burden if first-time offenders, once released, never offended again! What if we could take advantage of inmates' presence in prison to forever change their worldviews and related behaviors? What if we could dramatically reduce recidivism by altering behavior "on the inside"? Imagine the financial and emotional savings.

As everyone knows intuitively, no prisoner is going to do well on the outside if he or she chronically misbehaves on the inside. Thus, one leading indicator of post-release "likelihood to succeed" is behavior while incarcerated. Indeed, the entire "reduce recidivism" movement will be misguided if it focuses solely on post-release parole and probation programs.

We are, of course, aware of some successful post-release programs. For instance, the Delancey Street Foundation, headquartered in San Francisco, operates several residential rehabilitation houses in the United States and has processed some 11,000 former inmates through its programs. Former inmates spend several years helping to run Delancey's businesses while confessing their crimes and learning how to behave in society. But the average person in the Delancey Street program has had 18 convictions and has been incarcerated at least four times. As valuable as Delancey Street is to the former inmates (and all evidence suggests that it is very valuable), the program kicks in usually after the convicts are at their absolute bottom, and often after they have been convicted and released multiple times.[17]

Instead of waiting until former convicts are paroled and at rock bottom, we suggest that even more good can be done when the focus is placed on teaching inmates how to behave while incarcerated the first time. If that focus is not maintained, it is nearly certain that the status quo of high crime rates, high recidivism, and high taxes for prisons will continue.

If we can change behavior inside, we will reduce re-offences on the outside. Can we do it? That is the challenge we must meet. We are certainly not the first ones to address this issue, but just because it has not worked for some in the past is no reason not to try again. *While inmates are in prison the first time* (or in other ways under the care of the justice system the first time), we have to do something that will reduce the probability of re-offending. Cutting the recidivism rate by half, a third, or even a quarter would be a tremendous "win" for society. Can it be done? We think it can.

— **2** —

Attempts to Reform Prisoners

Historically, people thought of prisons as places where retribution and revenge were to be meted out to offenders. The criminals' pain, it was thought, would somehow bring justice to society. Through coercion—torture, hard labor, or solitary confinement, for example—it was thought that offenders would come to see the error of their ways and, upon release, live socially acceptable lives. Indeed, the term "penitentiary" came from the expectation that prisoners in solitary confinement would have time to become penitent and then commit to an upright life. These viewpoints have been present in most societies at some point in their histories, and they linger on in many.

However, most cultures have come to think of prisons as places where offenders should receive opportunities for mental or emotional reformation largely through moral persuasion rather than physical coercion—all the while being kept safely away from society, of course. Religion has sometimes been the vehicle for moral persuasion. There are thousands of instances of inmates who "got religion" while in prison because of active religious ministries by clergymen and women from all faiths determined to rehabilitate offenders with the "word of God." Indeed, modern prison reform in the West had its roots in the Quaker and Evangelical religions in the United Kingdom and in the Protestant "Social Gospel" movement in Europe and America.

In addition to religion, the intellectual community has often weighed in on prisoner reform. The English philosopher, Jeremy Bentham, for example, proposed numerous, innovative ways to construct prisons and handle prisoners, as did many others. From this philosophical foundation emerged a plethora of reform techniques: individual and group therapy, work-skills training, formal education leading to degrees while in prison, and many other similar reform and rehabilitation activities. Space does not allow us to review all of these techniques, but to provide a flavor of the overall movement, we will mention below two of the techniques currently receiving attention.

One is called restorative justice and was originally a faith-based approach. Beginning in Canada in the 1970s, restorative justice has now been considerably secularized and is found in prisons in many countries. Its core philosophy is that offenders are less likely to offend again if they are required to confront their offences in their entire social context. Thus, offenders are expected to meet their victims, listen to the impact of their crimes on the victims' lives and families, and then restore through cash or service that which they criminally removed from their victims. The focus is on the harm to the victims and society and on building relationships, rather than on the violation of the law, per se.

Does restorative justice work at reducing recidivism? The results are mixed. Perhaps one of the most successful programs is found in the community of Nanaimo, British Columbia, Canada. The Nanaimo Royal Canadian Mounted Police entered into a partnership in 1997 with a nonprofit organization, the Nanaimo Region John Howard Society. The program dealt primarily with young offenders (some under the age of 12) who had little or no prior criminal history. It was not a program for hardened, adult offenders. From 1998 to 2004, the program referred 960 offenders, two-thirds of whom were children and youth. Over six years, the program produced a recidivism rate of 14 percent, going down to an impressive 5 percent in the most recent four years.[18]

In Canberra, Australia, the percentage of violent-crime repeaters dropped 38 percent after restorative justice intervention,[19] while in New Zealand, reconviction rates dropped 4 percentage points for offenders treated with restorative justice techniques compared to a control group.[20]

However, a study by Hayes in 2005 was less positive. Hayes found, using U.S. data, that while violent offenders were less likely to re-offend after being included in some restorative justice programs, the same techniques seemed to have no effect on other criminals such as property offenders.[21] An earlier study by Hayes and Daly found no causal link between the use of restorative justice methods and reductions in offending.[22] Similarly disappointing results were found in two studies by Maxwell and Morris on youth offenders.[23]

Howard Zehr, sometimes called "the grandfather of the restorative justice movement," openly admitted to an audience at the University of Copenhagen Denmark that the early, glowing stories told by practitioners about the positive impact of restorative justice need to be tempered by reality — a reality that includes many instances of failure.[24]

The second technique receiving attention is called the 7 *Habits*. Could the 7 *Habits* approach, either by itself or together with other techniques, produce more consistently positive recidivism results? For some 20 years, the principles embedded in Stephen R. Covey's *The 7 Habits of Highly Effective People* (and versions of it modified for teens and children) have found their way into boardrooms and classrooms around the world. *CEO Magazine* named the 7 *Habits* "one of the two most influential business books of the twentieth century," and thousands of people support that ranking by offering testimonials to the positive impact of the 7 *Habits* on their lives. Indeed, the assertion that "the habits entirely changed my life!" is a common statement found in the records FranklinCovey (the company cofounded by Covey to promote the 7 *Habits*) keeps about the impact of its training programs on individuals. Is there reason to think the 7 *Habits* might work inside the walls of prisons? Could the 7 *Habits* improve the behavior of inmates while incarcerated and thereby improve their chances of having a successful release? Can the 7 *Habits* serve as leading indicators of reduced recidivism?

> Experiments with 7 *Habits* in prisons are taking place around the world.

As it happens, a number of experiments with the 7 *Habits* in prisons (or with offenders on alternative sentences) have been taking place around the world—some of them relatively unknown to FranklinCovey until recently. In the next few chapters, we will summarize those experiments and then decide if there is a case that can be made for the 7 Habits "on the inside" as a way of improving the behavior of inmates while incarcerated and thereby reducing recidivism when they are released.

3

7 Habits Programs for Adult Offenders
The 7 Habits *in Collier County, Florida*

Collier County in southwest Florida U.S.A. (2010 population: 331,800) is the largest county, geographically, in the state. Parks, nature preserves, and wildlife refuges, including portions of the Everglades and 37 miles of beach coastline facing the Gulf of Mexico, comprise over 800,000 acres of the county–and there are also 91 golf courses. Tourists flock to the county each winter season (when daytime temperatures are a balmy 75 degrees even in the coldest month), adding over 106,000 temporary visitors each year.

Public safety for the residents and tourists is handled by County Sheriff Kevin J. Rambosk and his team. Because most of the county (88 percent) is unincorporated into city boundaries, Sheriff Rambosk's work is critical for maintaining safety. Officers are assigned to six patrol districts, and special operations (SWAT, canine, marine, the bomb squad, mounted police, and others) are called in as needed. The sheriff's office also works closely with the Department of Homeland Security, Immigration and Customs Enforcement, the Florida Department of Law Enforcement, and the FBI, but most lawbreakers requiring incarceration are initially placed in the main county jail at Naples or the smaller jail at Immokalee Center.

Fortunately for Sheriff Rambosk's workload, some (about 25 percent) arrestees are found to be illegally present in the United States and are eventually handed over to Homeland Security. Another characteristic that helps the workload is that the crime rate in Collier County has been on the decline for the past decade; in 2000, there were about 4000 crimes per 100,000 inhabitants. Today, at 2027, it is almost half. This may be the result of a much slower pace of population growth, even a decline, in the county in the past several years.

Despite this trend, the sheriff's office handles thousands of calls each year and makes numerous jail bookings each day. The office responded to 633,426 calls from the public for help in 2007, for example. Illustrative of a single day's work at the sheriff's office, the records show that on February 28, 2010, 21 people were booked into the county jail. Four of them were women. The average age was 34, and the violations included driving while intoxicated, drug possession, theft, battery, and other charges. On some days, the office books 40 or more offenders, but on average, between 20 to 30 people are charged and booked into jail each day.

For Dr. Leo Mediavilla of Naples, Florida, these bookings presented an opportunity to do some good. Formerly an administrator for adult and community education programs in Florida, Dr. Mediavilla had taught *7 Habits* courses for the school system and for the sheriff's department. He believed that people's time in jail could be used to prepare them for a more useful and law-abiding life upon release. It would require the acquisition of two things: education, including practical training, and a new self-image.

After collaborative efforts with Collier County Public School staff and the Collier County Sheriff's Office jail administrators—including Chief Scott Salley, Commander Kevin McGowan, and Lieutenant Shirley Noya—the Administrator of Adult and Community Education, Robert Breitbard, applied for and was awarded a grant from the Florida Department of Education to conduct training programs in the county jail. The program thus created, with assistance from inmates, is called "Workshop 101" and is taught by Dr. Mediavilla and Buddy Schultheis. It includes General Educational Development (GED) training to help offenders obtain a high school diploma equivalency, learning activities from the Florida Ready to Work Program, and Florida Career CHOICES, as well as other skill-based training. Significantly, it also includes training in *The 7 Habits of Highly Effective People.*

Mediavilla believed that inmates, while incarcerated, needed to acquire a new self-image, a new self-paradigm. They also needed to be able to speak a common language in the cell blocks so that they could practice their new "selves" on each other. The 7 *Habits*, with its focus on "proactivity," "win-win problem solving," "synergy," and other behaviors, seemed like just the right thing. The goal was to have inmates, once released, be better prepared to succeed on the outside. After release, when they would be asked by a prospective employer if they had ever been convicted of a felony, they would have to say yes, but Mediavilla also wanted to prepare them with a portfolio of positive things they had accomplished while in jail—including the acquisition of a new mindset based on completion of the 7 *Habits* training program. This would give them something positive to tell a prospective employer, and it would give them the courage to keep trying until they completed their transition to life on the outside.

Mediavilla selected a version of the 7 *Habits* suite called "7 *Habits Associates.*" He taught the program to upper-level officials, to sheriff's deputies and, of course, to the inmates. At first, he admits, it was a challenge because of the "old school" mentality still residing in the minds of some people. By "old school," he meant the attitude that offenders should be punished, not "coddled." But as more people participated in Dr. Mediavilla's training, the level of resistance declined because of the apparent power of the program to change the behavior of inmates.

What were the results? Is there empirical evidence for the positive impact of the 7 *Habits* on recidivism and behavior in Collier County? According to jail records reviewed by Commander Kevin M. McGowan, 103 inmates received Workshop101/7 *Habits* training from 2009 to June 2010. Of the 103 graduates of the program, 15 re-offended after release, including 4 who committed felony offences (2 were violent). The other 11 committed misdemeanor crimes such as criminal traffic offences. Concludes Commander McGowan, "The result of this study of [program] participants reveals an 85 percent success rate." By "success rate," McGowan means the percentage of offenders who did not reoffend after release,

> Of the 103 graduates, only 4 re-committed felony offences compared to 27 for the 103 inmates in the non-7 *Habits* group.

or in other words, a recidivism rate of 15 percent (see Figure 3).

By contrast, when McGowan sampled 103 inmates who had not taken the Workshop 101 training, he found substantially different results: 37 of the general population of inmates had re-offended, including 27 who had committed felony offences (3 were violent); 10 had committed misdemeanor offences. The recidivism rate for this group was 36 percent, or more than double the 7 *Habits* group.

Fig. 3

Recidivism Rates for General Population Inmates vs. Workshop 101 / 7 *Habits* Graduates

	General Inmates	Workshop 101 Graduates
Total inmates studied	103	103
Felony offences	27	4
Violent offences*	3	2
Misdemeanors	10	11
Total re-offences	37	15
Recidivism rate	37%	15%

*Violent offences is a sub-category of felony offences. Source: Kevin M. McGowan, Collier County Sheriff's Office, July 2, 2010.

The data thus point in the right direction and suggest a positive influence of Workshop 101, including the 7 *Habits*. But there are a number of unanswered questions that will likely be answered with further research: Did the inmates re-offend in another jurisdiction? Were the inmates out long enough to really test the impact of the training? If they were sent to prison, did they take their 7 *Habits* lifestyle with them? And there are other methodological questions that need resolution, including questions about the composition of the matched pairs and the influence of the voluntary nature of Workshop 101 on the reported differences.

Despite these unanswered questions, the results point in the hoped-for direction. Of course, positive results do not happen without effort. Mediavilla, who holds an Ed.D in Educational Leadership from South Florida University, is determined to maintain a regular cycle of instruction for the inmates. He hangs 7 *Habits* posters on the walls of the Collier County Jail to help remind offenders of the principles they are trying to practice, and when offenders do written learning projects during the program, he posts some of the work on the walls as examples.

Is the program expensive? According to the sheriff's office, Workshop 101," including the 7 *Habits* training, is a "cost neutral" program. That is, while it requires a budget to acquire the teaching materials and run the program, the budget is repaid by improved behavior and the reduction in recidivism reported above.

> "It's amazing to see the transformation of these guys when they have the *7 Habits* as a tool to use when they need it." — Dr. Mediavilla

Significantly, Mediavilla has inmates/students co-teach with him as part of the program. They "teach to learn." He works with them behind the scenes to give them tips on appropriate body language for teachers. At the end of the training, the inmates are given a graduation certificate. The program recycles about every six weeks, so some of the offenders take the program more than once. If they are transferred from the county jail to a state or federal prison, some of them end up teaching the 7 *Habits* at their new location. Participation is voluntary and all types of crimes are represented, but for this particular program, extremely violent offenders are not admitted. All of the students are males, and a large percentage of them are Hispanics. There are between 25 to 48 in each group. Drug abusers are first sent to a recovery program and then, if they wish, are included in the 7 *Habits* course.

"It's amazing to see the transformation of these guys when they have the 7 *Habits* as a tool to use when they need it," says Mediavilla, or "Dr. M." as the inmates call him. "When they get into a fight, we remind them of one of the 7 *Habits* and have them talk about it. It's making a big difference in their lives."

"Workshop 101" includes training in a variety of skills, such as the knowledge normally gained from a GED program as well as the paradigm shift that comes from the 7 *Habits*. Which of these has the greater influence or which has no influence has not been studied. But those who have worked with the inmates hold that the practical training from the GED and other programs would not be sufficient to alter attitudes and self-images without the foundation of the 7 *Habits*. The 7 *Habits* is the activating or catalyzing force that motivates inmates to acquire and use the other kinds of training. Lets now look at another example.

The *7 Habits* in a California Women's Prison

"I was terrified of them at first," admitted a volunteer in a women's prison in California, U.S.A. "But I started asking them why they were in prison, and I discovered they were fabulous people."[25] Joan (a pseudonym because she wished to keep her service anonymous) started volunteering at the women's prison in 2006 as part of her commitment to a religious ministry for people in need. She was asked by prison officials to work with the 18- to 30-year old group, and started attending religious services with them in the prison and getting to know them. She learned that they had committed every type of crime imaginable, and many of them were in for life sentences.

Not long after she started working with the women, she was approached by two inmates—one in for murder, the other for theft—each of whom had already spent two decades in prison. They had read a copy of *The 7 Habits of Highly Effective People* they had found in the prison library. Learning that Joan had a FranklinCovey connection (she was a certified facilitator), they asked if she would set up a class to teach the 7 *Habits* to other women.

Joan agreed, arranging a schedule and acquiring training materials for a group of 20 interested women. The women were, she said, "like sponges." Every Sunday afternoon for several months, the group gathered for two hours to learn the 7 *Habits* and apply the principles to life inside. The women loved the classes, had a positive attitude about the entire process, and quickly spread the word to other women.

By the end of 2008, some 300 women had taken the classes. But Joan did not do all of the teaching. In fact, she only taught the first 36 women. The inmates who first proposed the idea received training to become "facilitators," and they became the official teachers of the 7 Habits course. The lifers were especially interested in having the younger group of short-term women take the 7 Habits to prepare them for the outside and to prevent them from coming back to prison. So committed were they to this form of "giving back" that they asked the warden to let them teach the 7 Habits as their prison job. They wrote some of their own teaching materials, organized graduation events for each class, and requested that Dr. Stephen R. Covey visit the prison and speak to the women.

One of the interesting aspects of this particular 7 Habits program in California is that it had little or no financial support from the prison administration. In fact, prison officials had little to do with it except giving permission for it to be taught. Initially, books and training materials were donated rather than purchased. When that generosity was tapped out, the program stopped for about six months. But demand from the inmates brought it back in mid-2009, again taught entirely by inmates.

> The program can be implemented on a limited budget.

Did it work? Because it was a more or less homegrown program, nobody thought about tracking all 300 women graduates to see if their behavior in prison had improved or to see if those out on parole actually stayed out. We have often found that those involved in promoting the 7 Habits to inmates fail to keep track of their successes. Joan comments, however, that women often came up to her and, with pride, reported that they had not received a behavior code write-up for several months "because you taught us not to be reactive, not to fight, but to talk it through." Joan also reports that within the group of younger women in the prison who had taken the 7 Habits, there was only one recidivist.

We know these are not the kind of empirical results that will convince prison administrators to try the 7 Habits in their prisons, but we can at least say a few positive things about the California experience:

- The women inmates loved the classes.
- The older inmates who taught the classes found great fulfillment in helping the younger inmates.
- Anecdotal evidence suggests a reduction in behavioral violations by those who took the course.
- Recidivism may have been reduced for 7 *Habits* "graduates" (but the evidence is anecdotal).
- The program can be implemented on a limited budget.

Hard evidence from this particular effort at using the 7 *Habits* on the inside is not yet available, but other experiments with actual recidivism data are being conducted.

The 7 Habits in Other Prison Settings

We know of other prisons—in Singapore, Florida, and Colorado—that merit additional study on the impact of the 7 *Habits*. In Singapore, the 7 *Habits* are taught to both adult and youth offenders at two locations. In the U.S. Federal Correctional Institution, Federal Prison Camp, in Miami, Florida, qualified inmates are offered the possibility of a 12-month sentence reduction if they complete 500 intensive treatment hours in the residential Drug Abuse Treatment Program. Called "I CAN," the treatment program consists of set courses that include, among others, *The 7 Habits of Highly Effective People.*"[26]

In Cañon City, Colorado, U.S.A, volunteers in some of the prisons have been training inmates in the 7 *Habits* for some 12 years. Former Director of Prisons for the State of Colorado, Jerry Gasko, first learned about *The 7 Habits of Highly Effective People* while serving in the United States Army in the 1980s.[27] In 1996, He decided to have the 7 *Habits* taught to the prison warden and directors at one of the facilities. Eventually, the program expanded to the inmates in several locations around the state in the form of an eight-week course. As of 2010, some 1500 inmates had graduated from the program.

The results to date have not been reported empirically (although a study is now underway), but tetstimonial evidence suggests solid improvements in behavior by 7 *Habits* inmates while incarcerated and a likely reduction in recidivism upon release. Whereas the Colorado results are only anecdotal at this point, empirical results from yet another experiment in Pennsylvania support the claims we are making for the value of the 7 *Habits* in reducing recidivism. Let us turn to that experiment.

— 4 —

Using the *7 Habits* to Reduce Juvenile Recidivism in the United States[28]

Judge Daniel B. Garrett, District Judge in Lancaster County, Pennsylvania, U.S.A., employs a unique approach with juvenile offenders in his courtroom. Here is what he does, in his own words:

"As part of alternative sentencing, I sentence juveniles to read *The 7 Habits of Highly Effective Teens* by Sean Covey and submit a report showing how this book has personally affected them. I do not want a rote regurgitation of what is in Chapters 1, 2, 3, etc.

"They are on initial probation for three months, during which time they are to read the book and submit their report. I then schedule a follow-up hearing, during which we discuss their report. This is a minimum of 30 minutes, sometimes lasting over an hour. My staff knows not to schedule too tight for these meetings. I emphasize that these changes in thinking and behavior are still fresh and will take time until they become habits! I will extend probation for individuals that I feel need some monitoring, such as for school attendance or fighting, as well as underage drinking. I then meet with them every 30 days for about 6 months.

"The recidivism rate for these juveniles has been **zero**!" (Emphasis in original.)

The juveniles in Judge Garrett's courtroom are usually between the ages of 15 and 17; some of them are single parents; many of them are in trouble because of underage drinking or driving while under the influence of alcohol; others are in court because of drugs. One girl, arrested and in court for her third underage drinking violation, started to read *Effective Teens* but "didn't think the book was going to do anything for me." By the time she wrote her book report for Judge Garrett, however, she apparently had changed her mind: "The book truly helped me. I used everything I read as a remedy for all the things I now admit I was wrong for doing; I am done with underage drinking."

Another juvenile who had struggled with low self-esteem and then had fallen into drinking to try to feel better about herself wrote a 12-page report and concluded with these words: "This book is one of the best books that I have ever read in my entire life. Reading [other] teens' stories on what they do when they feel depressed or upset helped me search and find other ways to control my emotions."

> The recidivism rate in Judge Garrett's courtroom is 2.5 times lower than the rest of Lancaster County.

The reports are due on Day 75 of their 90-day probations, and Judge Garrett reviews each written report carefully, correcting spelling mistakes, circling fragment sentences, and asking the writer to say more about this or that point. He also freely peppers the reports with his own handwritten comments: "Wonderful!" or "You are way ahead of most kids," or "Wonderful observation," or "OK, give me an example." He asks each juvenile offender to describe how the book relates to his or her personal life, and then he spends time with each juvenile in his courtroom with parents present, reviewing the report and getting the youth to verbalize their feelings about their past behaviors and future plans.

Judge Garrett strongly encourages the parents to read the book at the same time. "I always question the parents as to whether they have read the book and their child's report. I have been known to chastise those who have not."

Juveniles must also submit the book along with their report so that Judge Garrett can read the pages in the book that need to be filled in. He tells them that if their parent is also reading the book and they would like to keep their answers confidential, they can put their responses on a separate sheet of paper.

Since the initial results in 2007, Judge Garrett has had a few juveniles (4 out of 35) return for second offences, but the recidivism rate as of 2009 in his courtroom was still *2.5 times lower* than Lancaster County overall: 11 percent compared to 28 percent, and over 3 times lower than other counties such as Fayette (Pittsburgh) where the recidivism rate was 36 percent.[29]

We wonder what the impact on society would be if Judge Garrett's *7 Habits* approach were implemented in juvenile courtrooms everywhere? We wonder what taxpayers would say to their governments if they learned there was a program available that could reduce recidivism by 2.5 to 3 times? What if recidivism everywhere could be reduced to 11 percent, as happened in Judge Garrett's jurisdiction when he used the *7 Habits*?

As it happens, other judges are also experimenting with the *7 Habits*. Let's see what they are doing.

5

The Chrysalis Program™ and the *7 Habits* in the United Kingdom

Applying the Benefits of the Boardroom to the Prison Cell[30]

David Apparicio is a justice of the peace (magistrate) in Northampton, England. After talking with offenders and fellow colleagues at all levels of the criminal justice system to learn why individuals offend and then re-offend, David Apparicio realized that the gap between what society sees as acceptable and how offenders actually behave is addressed by the criminal-justice system in a very different way from how performance gaps are treated in the business world.

In the criminal-justice system, as David Apparicio sees it, the primary reason for intervention in a sentencing situation appears to be to administer punishment, whereas in the business world, when there is a performance gap between expectations and behavior, leaders attempt to close that gap through the provision of knowledge, skills, practice, behaviors, and values that move the individual to the desired state of performance. David Apparicio knows what happens in the business world because, in addition to his work as a justice of the peace (which is a voluntary appointment), he works in senior leadership and development roles for the Royal Mail. For 20 years, he has implemented a variety of employee-development approaches, finding that some of them produced measurable impacts on the attitudes, behavior, and performance of employees.

Yet, as a justice of the peace, he found himself frustrated by the criminal-justice system's unwillingness to provide developmental focused sentencing interventions—tactics that would address the core beliefs and values of offenders as well as equip them with the skills they would need to gain sustainable employment upon release. He wondered, "Why not tap into the wealth of proven corporate sector behavioral-change programs and merge them with the best practices from Offender Management Services?"

What was needed, as he saw it, was an integrated, high-quality program that was not bound by low societal expectations of the capabilities of offenders. Of the corporate training programs he had worked with, the one David Apparicio favored was *The 7 Habits of Highly Effective People*. He therefore chose the philosophy of the *7 Habits* to be the keystone of his work with youth offenders. Thus was born the "Chrysalis Program," a single, holistic human-development program deliverable in 12 modules, with the end in mind of returning employable, productive individuals to society and ameliorating the impact of crime on affected families.

> Why not use the best practices from the corporate boardroom to improve behavior in the cell blocks?

The program he developed addressed, for the first time in his courtroom, the causes of re-offending. His integrated end-to-end offender-management programs focused on development and rehabilitation so that offenders were provided with the skills, knowledge, and behaviors that would enable them to gain sustainable employment and feel that they are part of society upon release from the criminal-justice system.

David Apparicio is very realistic about what the program can and cannot do. He knows that the approach will not remove re-offending completely. But he believes that by rehabilitating those individuals exhibiting serious criminal and antisocial behaviors, other youth in the community will be positively influenced. Thus, the offenders of the past will become the change agents and role models of positive behavior in the future. The result, he hopes, will be a reduction in crime and antisocial behavior as well as the creation of safer communities.

How the Program Works

According to Magistrate Apparicio, the Chrysalis Program's Behavioral Framework emphasizes offender self-awareness, personal effectiveness, and motivation to own and drive personal change in behavior. It uses proven principles known for their ability to encourage change. It provides offenders with a holistic development program that is usually the bastion of senior and executive management in the corporate domain. It then combines the development program with probation services in order to fully support personal behavioral change.

In the program, offenders are supported through an integrated 12-month behavioral-development plan that uses work placements, mentoring, community challenge projects, a discovery journal, intermodule activity, and leading experts to inspire long-lasting personal development and transformation. In addition, the Chrysalis Program has been tailored in the UK First Step for use with Drug and Alcohol Rehab Unit clients. "Chrysalis Lite," the addiction-recovery program supports individuals as they move away from drug or alcohol dependency. The Chrysalis Lite programme was independently evaluated by Teesside University whose Research Fellow wrote in conclusion:

> There is nothing about a caterpillar that tells you it's going to become a butterfly.
>
> —*Chrysalis Program Motto*

"Overall, participants reported learning a lot on the programme.... It had helped them understand their problems and also helped to believe that they can make changes.... Steps should be taken to ensure that the Chrysalis Programme becomes imbedded into the Drug & Alcohol Rehab services...and mechanisms put in place to ensure its availability to clients...."

The effectiveness of the Chrysalis Lite program has meant that it has been further developed for use with prisoners while in custody as a short-duration high-impact intervention delivered over six weeks.

The Chrysalis Program is (through Edexcel) a fully accredited Level 2 BTEC qualification in WorkSkills.

Offenders attend 18 days of learning divided into 12 development modules:

Module 1 - Know Thyself

Module 2 – *The 7 Habits of Highly Effective People*

Module 3 – Interpersonal & Communication Skills

Module 4 – Health & Wellness (Drug & Alcohol Awareness)

Module 5 – Presenting Yourself

Module 6 – Motivational Event

Module 7 – Numeracy

Module 8 – Personal Leadership

Module 9 – Thinking Differently

Module 10 – Change & Cultural Diversity

Module 11 – Business Enterprise

Module 12 – Your Role in the Community

Modules 1–3 are particularly critical to the success of the Chrysalis Program, says David Apparicio, and Module 2 is when FranklinCovey's *7 Habits* principles are introduced.

Status of the Program to Date

The program started in late 2007, and by 2009 some 48 classes in four prisons with 10 inmates per program were underway. Inmates from ages 14 to 60 have participated to date, but those ages 18 to 24 are the main target group. The costs of the program are personally funded by David Apparicio and Supported by the Chrysalis Foundation, established as a Social Enterprise, the charity arm of the effort.

As of October 2009, over 100 young offenders have taken the Chrysalis course at Her Majesty's Prison and Young Offenders Institution in Reading, Berkshire, England. HMP/YOI Reading holds offenders who are between the ages of 18 and 21 years. They are young offenders who have committed such offences as robbery, drug violations, and sexual crimes, with violence against persons and theft as well as handling stolen goods constituting the majority of their offences.

An additional 12 offenders have taken the course at Her Majesty's Prison, High Down, in Sutton, Surrey. Thirty people have also participated in the First Step Drug and Alcohol Rehab program, and 15 offenders from Preston Probation in Lancashire have participated. In addition, 25 members of staff have taken the training. All of this has been provided by 14 trained facilitators.[31]

The United Kingdom has established two years as the cutoff for measuring re-offending, so at the time this book was written, the program had not been running long enough to fit within the government's measures of re-offending. But prison officials in Reading were so impressed with the improvement in inmate behavior of those who had completed the program that they introduced Chrysalis to expand to additional prisons in south central England, and at press time, discussions were underway to take the program to one of Europe's largest prisons as well as to a county police service to support probationers in their post-release care.

So far, we have reviewed instances of behavioral change and dramatically reduced recidivism in systems where the 7 *Habits* have been taught. But exactly how do individual inmates integrate the 7 *Habits* into their personal lives? For that, we turn to the stories of Michael Santos and Weldon Long.

6

Individual Inmate Application of the *7 Habits* for Behavioral Change
Michael Santos

For nearly two years, high school graduate Michael Santos sold cocaine through a small network of friends in Miami and Seattle. The cocaine earned him hundreds of thousands of dollars—and a 45-year sentence in federal prison.[32]

In the late 1980s, when Michael was still adjusting to life in prison, a friend recommended Stephen R. Covey's *The 7 Habits of Highly Effective People*. He found a copy of the book in the prison library and read it several times, memorizing parts of it. The book had "a profound effect," reports Carole, a high school friend whom Michael later married while in prison. "He lives and breathes the *7 Habits* in everything he thinks, says, and does." Michael is currently in his twenty-second year of confinement; but, says his wife, "the lessons he embraced in the book helped him form the foundation for his extraordinary journey."

And what was that journey? Michael decided that the *7 Habits* were principles he could use in prison to help him make something meaningful out of his time behind bars, and he came to believe they could help other inmates too. In 1995, he asked his prison administrators if he could teach the *7 Habits* to other inmates in a formal classroom setting under the Adult Continuing Education program. He designed the lessons to be taught in 10 two-hour segments. Upon completion, prison administrators were to issue certificates.

The prison officials agreed, and as of 2009, Michael had taught 50 courses, with 20 to 30 inmates in each course, for a total participation of well over 1000 inmates. Michael emphasizes making something useful out of prison life rather than focusing only on using the *7 Habits* to get out. He believes that if inmates can learn to be good citizens on the inside, they will be good citizens on the outside—a belief consistent with our assertion. He also believes that the prison system, as it currently exists, does not encourage personal growth by inmates, but instead produces apathy and discouragement. As Michael sees it, the *7 Habits* are antidotes to that.

Michael Santos has been held in six different federal prisons, and with good time and parole, he could be released in 2013 at age 49. With the *7 Habits* as his foundation, he has not wasted his time. He has earned a bachelor's degree from Mercer University and a master's degree from Hofstra University, and was the valedictorian speaker of his prison graduating class. His graduation message to his fellow inmates was to make goals and stick with them. He has authored four non-fiction books on prison life, including *Inside: Life Behind Bars in America* (published by St. Martin's Press in 2007), and he has created a prison blog that generates comments from around the country. One section of his blog, "The Seven Habits of Highly Successful Prisoners," includes a summary of each of the *7 Habits* and describes how that particular habit can be applied to prison life.

"Dr. Covey's book has inspired me, and I rely upon it to teach others," says Michael. "It is my contention that the individuals who succeed upon release adjust differently from those who meander through terms of confinement. The trouble prisoners have, my experience suggests, is in sustaining motivation. To overcome this obstacle, I use many examples in each lesson to describe how incremental victories along the long journey open new opportunities that would not have otherwise become possible. In leading prison classes, I have found that class participants respond well to these types of examples.

"I am convinced that prisoners need to believe that thinking proactively can position them for success. Everyone in prison wants to succeed upon release, but two out of three prisoners fail. Those of us inside must anticipate the obstacles that await us and think creatively about how we can overcome them."

Michael believes he knows the struggles other inmates have in making prison a positive experience. "I show how a proactive adjustment, a deliberate adjustment, can lead to a meaningful life." He helps other inmates create résumés and then assists them in developing a network of potential employers who would be willing to hire them when their prison terms are up.

Michael's published descriptions of prison life are not universally heralded. Some think he has been too harsh on prison officials and that he should be more grateful than he appears to be for the opportunity to obtain college and graduate degrees while in prison. Others believe that he has not yet paid back enough for the harm his drugs did to innocent people in the past. What is clear to everyone, however, is that Michael Santos has used his time well while in prison, helping develop himself and helping others to develop. The foundation for that optimistic and proactive approach came from *The 7 Habits of Highly Effective People*.

Weldon Long

High school dropout Weldon Long spent twenty years of his life drinking, doing drugs, stealing, lying, and destroying his business, marriage, and family relationships. But after 13 years in federal and state prisons and halfway houses, he emerged transformed.[33]

In fact, after prison, he worked hard and discovered he had a knack for selling and motivating others to sell. Today he is the CEO of a multimillion-dollar speaking and personal-development company, and he has a good relationship with his wife and son. How did he make the transformation?

"...I read Stephen Covey's *The 7 Habits of Highly Effective People*. Like many of the books I picked up in the early days of my recovery, it chose me more than I chose it. As I began reading, I felt as though something significant was going to happen. For the first time, I was actually thinking about my life—what it meant, if anything, and what I was doing with it.

"When I read Covey's discussion of the 'personality ethic' versus the 'character ethic,' a light clicked on in my head. The personality ethic described me perfectly. It defined a lifestyle that was based on pretending and getting people to believe I was something that I was not.

"The first thing I had to do to change my life was to quit pretending I was someone I was not. I had to accept that I was a common criminal, a liar, and a thief.

"Understanding and accepting that I embodied the personality ethic was much easier than instantly living the character ethic that Covey described.

"Understanding who was responsible for my circumstances and quality of life was critically important to building a healthy, productive life. I had to accept that I had a choice in how I responded to the challenges I faced. It was equally important to understand that the quality of my responses would determine the quality of my life."

During his years in prison, Weldon obtained a college education and read other books on self-improvement. But what is significant is that he used his time in prison to practice living a good life. When he was finally released, he was ready. As he says, "I was determined to live honestly in prison as practice for living honestly in the real world."

> I was determined to live honestly in prison as practice for living honestly in the real world.

This is precisely the benefit of the *7 Habits* on the inside: it gives prisoners something to work on while incarcerated that will become of immediate use to them in prison and then later, upon release. Weldon Long's and Michael Santos' life stories confirm our belief that the *7 Habits* provide the basis for fundamental change.

~ 7 ~

What Have We Learned? Where Do We Go From Here?

In this short tour of the "prison problem," we have learned that recidivism, which hovers around 50 to 60 percent in most countries, constitutes a tremendous financial and social burden on society. Other worthwhile causes in society are denied funds because so many tax dollars are spent locking up criminals again and again and again. We have also seen that, unless changes are made in the rehabilitation system, there will be even more repeat offenders in the future because, in most countries, more and more people are being sent to prison in the first place, and not enough is happening to keep them from re-offending. In most cases, efforts to monitor criminals after release (probation and parole), have not improved the recidivism rate. It is our assertion that for the repeat-offence rate to decline, prisoners must change behavior *while they are in prison the first time.* This would require them to make a change in their worldview, and that change, we believe, is mapped out for them in the 7 *Habits.* We believe that the more deeply inmates are immersed in the mind-set of the 7 *Habits* while in prison, the better their behavior will be in and out of prison.

A number of experiments with the 7 *Habits* are underway around the world for both youth and adult offenders that, we believe, add empirical substance to our claim. One of those experiments, as we have seen, is in the courtroom of Judge Daniel B. Garrett in Pennsylvania, U.S.A., who has produced a youth recidivism rate of just 11 percent, or

2.5 times lower than similar courtrooms in surrounding communities. He did this on his own initiative using the concepts of *The 7 Habits of Highly Effective Teens*.

A more complex program is underway in the United Kingdom under the guidance of Justice of the Peace David Apparicio, who is using the *7 Habits* with drug and alcohol offenders as well as other types of offenders. We have also heard of *7 Habits* training being given in both an adult prison and a boys' home in Singapore, as well as in a prison in the Czech Republic, in a federal prison in Miami, Florida, and in the Oregon State Penitentiary in the U.S.A.

Some of these experiments are small and have been underway for only a short time, but in Colorado, U.S.A., a more extensive program has been underway for the past 12 years. Over 1,500 offenders, both male and female, have taken the *7 Habits* course. The impact of these courses on recidivism awaits the results of a larger study now underway, but movement to date seems to be in the hoped-for direction.

We have also learned that once inmates are exposed to the *7 Habits*, they often have a strong desire to share the concepts with other inmates. One such inmate, Michael Santos, has now taught the *7 Habits* to over 1000 prisoners over his 22-year prison career, and another, Weldon Long, used the *7 Habits* to make substantial changes in his behavior while in prison—changes which, upon release, helped him create his own multimillion-dollar company and establish successful family relationships. We have also learned that the *7 Habits* are easily absorbed by inmates; they are not hard principles to "sell." We have seen, for example, that adult women in a prison in California were uniformly enthusiastic about the value of the *7 Habits* training they had received.

In some of the experiments we have reviewed, solid statistical data were not collected; in other cases, we have the benefit of empirical evidence. We know that there was a statistically significant change in self-perception and perception of the prison system by women who completed the *7 Habits* course in California, and we know that recidivism dropped 2.5 times for offenders taking Judge Garrett's *7 Habits* training.

We wish we could report that all over the world, inmates who had taken the *7 Habits* course while in prison never re-offended and never returned to prison. Given human nature, it is highly unlikely that we would ever be able to make such an announcement. We also know that we have more research ahead of us to more fully verify the claims we and others are making about the *7 Habits*. But we believe the findings summarized in this book make a strong enough case for the beneficial value of the *7 Habits* to justify their widespread experimentation in prisons. Imagine the savings in tax dollars if recidivism declined by 2.5 times everywhere, as in Pennsylvania.

We also believe that the savings from reduced recidivism will more than pay for the cost of training inmates, guards, and other prison officials in the *7 Habits*. There may be prison officials whose budgets are so tight that they feel they cannot attempt the training. We urge them to reconsider, because making that decision will do nothing but guarantee the continuation of the status quo—and that would be intolerable for everyone.

Notes

1. Roy Walmsley, comp., *World Prison Population List,* 8th ed., International Centre for Prison Studies, King's College, London, 2009.
2. Justice Policy Institute Report: The Punishing Decade, & U.S. Bureau of Justice Statistics Bulletin, NCJ 219416—Prisoners in 2006.
3. "Recidivism of Prisoners Released in 1994," U.S. Department of Justice, Bureau of Justice Statistics, www.ojp.usdoj.gov/bjs/ (accessed September 2009).
4. David Apparicio, Magistrate, telephone interview, June 17, 2009.
5. *Forum on Corrections Research*, Correctional Service of Canada (1993), 5, 3.
6. "Examining the Unexamined: Recidivism Among Female Offenders," *Forum on Corrections Research*, Correctional Service of Canada (1993) 5, 3.
7. "FBI Data Show Violent Crime Dropped in 2008," *Deseret News*, September 15, 2009.
8. *Crime in the United States, Uniform Crime Reports*, 1996, Federal Bureau of Investigation, U.S. Department of Justice, September 28, 1997.
9. M. Chambers, B. Ullmann, and I. Waller, *Less Crime, Lower Costs: Implementing Effective Early Crime Reduction Programmes in England and Wales*, 2009.
10. "Criminal Offending, Social and Financial Exclusion, and Civil Legal Aid Fact Sheet," Legal Services Research Centre, 2009. http://www.lsrc.org.uk/publications/FactSheetCriminalOffend_July2009.pdf (accessed September 2009).
11. Lauren E. Glaze and Thomas P. Bonczar, *Probation and Parole in the United States, 2006*, U.S. Department of Justice, Bureau of Justice Statistics, 2007.
12. *Salem-News* "Governor Establishes Inmate Re-Entry Council," June 4, 2007.
13. "One in 100: Behind Bars in America 2008," Pew Charitable Trust, February 2008.

[14] "Senate Votes to Cut Prison Spending," *The Times Herald*, Associated Press, September 30, 2009.

[15] *St. Louis Post-Dispatch* (Missouri), "Reengineer Prisons: Illinois' Prisons Are Overpopulated and Understaffed," guest editorial, July 30, 2009.

[16] *Los Angeles Times*, "Lower Dropout Rate and Have Less Crime," September 24, 2009. See also http://www.smbgc.org/main.asp?id=37 (accessed February 18, 2010).

[17] *London Financial Times*, June 19–20, 1999, as per www.delanceystreetfoundation.org.

[18] "Nanaimo Restorative Justice: A Community Initiative," September 2004.

[19] Lawrence Sherman, Heather Strang, and Daniel Woods, "Recidivism Patterns in the Canberra Reintegrative Shaming Experiments (RISE)," 2000, 12.

[20] "A Summary of New Zealand Court-Referred Restorative Justice Pilot: Evaluation," Crime and Justice Research Centre, Victoria University, 2005.

[21] Hennessey Hayes, "Assessing Reoffending in Restorative Justice Conferences," *Australian and New Zealand Journal of Criminology* (2005) 38, 1: 77–102.

[22] Hennessey Hayes and Kathleen Daly, "Youth Justice Conferencing and Reoffending," *Justice Quarterly* (2003) 20: 757.

[23] Gabrielle Maxwell and Allison Morris, "Family Group Conferences and Reoffending," in G. Maxwell and A. Morris, eds., *Restorative Justice for Juveniles: Conferencing, Mediation, and Circles*, 2002.

[24] Jakob V. H. Holtermann, *Everything You Always Wanted to Know About Restorative Justice*, Ph.D. Thesis, Roskilde University, July 29, 2009.

[25] Telephone interviews with "Joan" September 2009.

[26] Federal Bureau of Prisons, http://www.bop.gov/locations/institutions/mia/MIA_aohandbook.pdf (accessed 6.22.10)

[27] Jerry Gasko, interviews, May 12 and May 24, 2009 by telephone and in Salt Lake City, Utah.

[28] This chapter, slightly modified for this book, appeared originally as "Reducing Juvenile Recidivism," FranklinCovey Center for Advanced Research, May 2009, www.franklincoveyresearch.org.

[29] David E. Kalist and Daniel Y. Lee, "Measuring and Analyzing Juvenile Recidivism in Rural and Urban Pennsylvania," Department of Economics, Shippensburg University of Pennsylvania, January 2009.

[30] Adapted from a report by David Apparicio, October 2009. See also http://www.chrysalisprogramme.com/. For direct information, contact telephone: +44(0)7801 033157/(0)7801 438140; email: davidapparicio@harnessingpotential.co.uk; website: http://www.chrysalisprogramme.com/; address: 485 Wellingborough Road, Abington, Northampton, Northants, NN33HN, England.

[31] Pat Watson, "Evaluation of the Chrysalis Lite Programme: First Step," University of Teeside School of Health and Social Care, 2009.

[32] Information for this section came from several email communications from Michael and Carole Santos in June 2009, as well as from Internet blogs maintained by Michael Santos.

[33] Information for this section is from Weldon Long, *The Upside of Fear: How One Man Broke the Cycle of Prison, Poverty, and Addiction*, Austin, Texas: Greenleaf Book Group Press, 2009.

Index

A

adult offenders– 12, 36
Australia– 12

B

Buddy Schultheis– 16
budgets for prisons– 7

C

California– 8, 20, 21, 37
Canada– 5, 12
Cañon City– 22
CEO– 13, 34
Chrysalis Program– 28, 29, 30
coercion– 11
Collier County, Florida– 15, 16, 17, 18, 19
Colorado– 22, 23, 37
cost of crime– 6, 8
crime rate– 4, 6, 9
crimes against persons– 6
Czech Republic– 37

D

Daniel B. Garrett– 24, 25, 26, 36, 37
David Apparicio– 27, 28, 29, 30, 37
Denmark– 13

E

England– 4, 5, 27, 30, 31
Europe– 11, 31

F

facilitators– 21, 31
Fayette County– 26
First Step Drug and Alcohol Rehab Unit– 29
Florida– 15, 16, 19, 22, 37
FranklinCovey– 13, 20, 30

G

GED– 16, 19, 20
guards– 6, 38

H

Howard Zehr– 13

I

I CAN– 22

J

Jeremy Bentham– 12
Jerry Gasko– 22
justice system– 2, 7, 9, 27, 28

K

Kevin J. Rambosk– 15
Kevin McGowan– 16

L

Lancaster County– 24, 25, 26
Leo Mediavilla– 16

M

Miami– 32
Michael Santos– 31, 32, 33, 34, 35, 37
motor vehicle thieves– 4

N

Nanaimo Royal Canadian Mounted Police– 12
New Zealand– 12

O

Offender Management Services– 28
offenders– 3, 4, 5, 6, 7, 8, 9, 11, 12, 13, 24, 27, 28, 29, 30, 31, 36, 37
Oregon– 7, 37
Oregon State Penitentiary– 37

P

parole– 6, 7, 9, 21, 33, 36
penitentiary– 11
Pennsylvania– 24, 36, 38
prisoner-education programs– 7, 8
probation– 7, 9, 24, 29, 36

R

Reading, Berkshire, England– 30
recidivism– 3, 4, 6, 7, 9, 10, 12, 13, 14, 22, 24, 25, 26, 31, 36, 37, 38
recidivism rate– 6, 7, 10, 12, 24, 25, 26, 36
rehabilitation– 6, 9, 12, 28, 36
religion– 11
repeat offenders– 8, 36
Restorative justice– 12
Robert Breitbard– 16

S

Scott Salley– 16
Sean Covey– 2, 24
Seattle– 32
Shirley Noya– 16
Singapore– 37
Stephen R. Covey– 13, 21, 32, 33, 34, 35
Sutton, Surrey, England– 31

T

taxes for prisons– 9
The 7 Habits of Highly Effective People– 13, 20, 28, 30, 32, 34

U

United Kingdom– 6, 11, 27, 29, 31, 37
United States– 3, 4, 5, 6, 7, 8, 9
University of Copenhagen– 13
U.S. Department of Justice– 4
Utah– 47

V

victims– 4, 6, 12
violent crime– 6, 12

W

warden– 21
Weldon Long– 31, 34, 35, 37
Workshop 101– 16, 18, 19

Y

youth offenders– 13, 28

About FranklinCovey

FranklinCovey (NYSE: FC) is the global consulting and training leader in the areas of strategy execution, customer loyalty, leadership, and individual effectiveness. Clients include 90 percent of the Fortune 100, more than 75 percent of the Fortune 500, thousands of small and midsize businesses, as well as numerous government entities and educational institutions. FranklinCovey has 46 direct and licensee offices providing professional services in 147 countries.

FranklinCovey offers training in the following areas:

- Leadership Development
- The 7 Habits
- Time Management
- Customer Loyalty
- Strategy Consulting
- Communication
- Project Management
- Diversity
- Sales Performance

For more information, go to www.franklincovey.com/tc.

About the Center for Advanced Research

The Center for Advanced Research conducts independent investigations into the impact of FranklinCovey training and consulting activities on individuals and organizations. The research staff and its advisory board constitute a team of dedicated professionals with experience in survey design, statistical analysis, and research methodologies. To access the Center's research library, see www.franklincoveyresearch.org.

About the Author

Fulbright Scholar Dr. Dean W. Collinwood holds a Ph.D. from the University of Chicago and a M.Sc. from the University of London. Before joining FranklinCovey as Executive Director of the Center for Advanced Research, he was Research Professor of Management and Director of the Center for International Business Education Research in the David Eccles School of Business at the University of Utah, U.S.A. Early in his academic career, he taught criminology at the College of the Bahamas in Nassau and later taught inmates at a medium-security prison in Illinois. He and his wife Kathleen, an attorney, live near Salt Lake City, Utah, U.S.A.